3rd Hour

Before The

Change

3rd Hour

Before The

Change

Jasmine Pennix

3rd Hour Before The Change

All rights reserved © 2019 by Jasmine Pennix

This is a work is based upon a series of events in my life.

Printed and distributed in the United States of America.

Author: Jasmine Pennix

jazzfromchi@yahoo.com

ISBN: 978-0-578-61974-3
LCCN: TBD

DEDICATION

In dedication to my friend, mentor, teacher, and the father-figure I wish I had. You were all that to me and some. If you only knew how blessed I was to know you. I'm very thankful that you came into my life at the right time.

I love you and you are greatly missed, William Omar "Chap" Daurham. Chazap Forever!

R.I.P. Grandma Jones, Lorenzo Beamon, TDG, Eric Davis, Nippsey, Bill, Danny, & Evon Roberson.

R.I.P. Dalpin and Cousin Tim

Chapter 1

The understanding of a positive turn around everywhere can be summed up like this: *an ounce of prevention is better than a pound of cure.* A Benjamin Franklin quote I was introduced to by Freeway Rick Ross.

An essential concept of this saying of exploring its explicit significance is: if we take several steps back to observe the behavior of all, many situations can be fairly, properly, and safely resolved. Not because one is viewed as a *leader* or *role model*, but to acknowledge that no university, college, high school, middle school, elementary school, kindergarten or preschool, or daycare will allow inappropriate and harmful behavior from an elderly person down to a toddler. We must learn not to underestimate his/her age to excuse any of their unkindly behavior or actions from the wrongfully accused – which is we, the people of the world. We, *the people of the world*, can sometimes be the wrongfully accused.

On April 20th of 2016, my life changed when a juvenile teenager, at the Milwaukee, WI high school I worked at, unlawfully attacked me, bringing harm to my life and turning my world upside down. The entire violent situation was captured and viewed on news outlets and social media for all to see. Confronted by this teenager, I was forced to defend myself from a troubled juvenile delinquent whose height and stature, almost coincided with mine. Because of the things he was able to get away with in the past, I believe he felt like he could do and get away with everything in his life. He had a sense of feeling untouchable, a millennial bully towards everyone. I wasn't the only adult that he felt he could conquer, as a few months prior, it was said that he brutally hospitalized another adult.

What I thought would be a normal day at my place of employment would turn to be one of the most painful times of my life. But when I look back on it, maybe it was all doomed to happen. It's ironic to me how April 20th was considered a holiday for marijuana users according to many of the students where I worked. On this faithful day of this run-in began my ruins. I had been in mourning for a few weeks due to the passing of two people close to me, one of my relatives and one of my very close friends.

Maybe slightly mentally distracted, the confrontation between myself and the juvenile caught me off guard.

While hindsight is 20/20, I realize that not once did the school administration provide me enough preventative insight into this juvenile teenager's past inappropriate behavior or previous incidents. They did not provide me with any type of strategic training method so that I would be able to handle the juvenile behavior in a safe and professional manner. The student had recently served in a detention center and was released on the Monday prior to the incident. There was no preventative measure put in place to counteract any future incidents with the student as he was known for being destructive and violent when he didn't get his way. And here it is, two days later, on a Wednesday and he attacks me. The school board was

4

also aware of the student's history, and I believe they should have put in place tactics before he returned back to the educational institution.

Information was introduced from law enforcement about the teenager's long rap sheet to the school and school board. I was shocked that the school board didn't do much or was not concerned about me being incarcerated for defending myself against the student's violent ways. When I was released from the county jail around midnight after three days of inhumane conditions that no one should encounter criminal or not, guilty or not, a camera crew from the local news were outside to get an exclusive interview of my unfortunate mishap. But I'd soon come to realize that the local media wasn't there to get my wrongful incarceration interview from my point-of-view of the incident; they were there to sensationalize the entire ordeal. I just wanted to go home. I was desperately trying to get away from the media; I began walking quickly from the county building to where my girlfriend at the time was waiting to drive me away from the chaotic scene.

As I was walking back towards my girlfriend's car, I began to think back to the dreadful week leading up to the incident between the student and me. That Monday, it was a regular day like any other day. I left school at 3:40 pm that day. There were a bunch of kids running away from the school, and the assistant principal had a bullhorn instructing the students. I wasn't paying much attention to what was being said, as I was more concerned about ending my day. As I was leaving school, the assistant principal asked me if I recognized any of the students that were running away from the school. Not thinking much about it, I rattled off the names and went on about the rest of my afternoon. Unbeknownst to me, I'd just implicated myself as a snitch to the students. Apparently, the students were ditching the seventh hour class period, and the assistant principal began to yell their names through the bullhorn. Unfortunately, this is where my problems started with the juvenile, as he was one of the students whose name was amongst the named names.

I remember that following Wednesday, the day of the incident that would forever change my life, I was in the basement of the gym hanging out with other staff. I remember flirting with a pretty lady who was there for the career day event the school

7

was having. I quickly remember that I had to substitute for another teacher who was away on a class field trip. I had to stay back and keep the students who were unable to attend the field trip due to their behavior. When I entered the classroom, it seemed to be an easy session until other students from other classrooms began to pour in. These were the students that I'd happened to *snitch on* two days prior.

The student that I would later have the incident with began to make some derogatory remarks about one of the other teachers in the school, a Middle Eastern teacher. The student was making jokes attempting to make the other students laugh. As he continued to disturb the classroom, I began to reprimand him and told him to chill out.

"Fuck you! I'll whip your ass." He said to me.

Slightly taken aback, I approached the student who was seated and demanded that he leave the classroom.

"Get the fuck out my face!" He screamed at me.

I asked him to leave the classroom again, to which he then stood up and began to invade my personal space. There was another student in the classroom who attempted to get in between us, but by this time, there was too much going on to stop the escalation of the incident. There was another substitute teacher who happened to walk past the classroom, and he witnessed the commotion. However, he didn't intervene; he just stood there, watching the two of us goes go back and forth with words. Soon I stopped myself and walked away. I walked over to the classroom phone to call for school security, but unfortunately, they were on lunch at the time. I had to figure out how to handle this unruly student on my own. This seemed to anger the student even more. He then approached me again and started to try and fight me. I put a chair between us to try and diffuse him, but it didn't work. Then suddenly, he did the unspeakable and spits in my face. "Snitch!" He snarls at me and then kicks me in my leg.

And this is when all the madness began. In a rage, I grabbed him and threw him over the tables to restrain him to the floor. I handle him the best way I could. I had to match his aggression; otherwise, he would have continued assaulting me, thinking he was above me. The classroom became very chaotic. Word of the classroom incident spread quickly to school security, who was apparently in the building but quickly ended their lunch. Soon they appeared into the classroom to break up the fight. As security was restraining me from the student, most of the other students began to turn on me and threatened that they were going to jump me. The juvenile ferociously began to try to fight me again. I was so angry, and all I knew was that I needed to protect myself from these students.

As the security pulled both of us into the hallways of the school, the student was still trying to attack me. I had never seen anything like it. It's like this teenager wasn't afraid of anything or anyone – and that was the scary part.

Once everything cooled down, I needed to go for a walk to cool off. When I was able to calm down some, I went to the principal's office to speak to the assistant principal to tell my side of the story. The juvenile happened to be in the office as well and began spewing words at me that reflected his still heightened anger towards me. Soon the school principal would join in on the conversation, and shortly after the police entered into the room as well.

When the police came into the room, they stood as asked me to recount my side of the incident again. I was sure that after hearing my side that they would understand why I chose to defend myself. So you would understand my shock when they proceeded to handcuff me and read me my Miranda Rights. And to make matters worse, as I'm standing there in handcuffs, the principal of the school handed me a letter, which I would later find out that it was a termination of the employment with the school effective immediately. I was astonished that she hadn't taken the time to hear me out fully. It was as if she wanted to wash her hands with it completely, and it was her attempt to separate the school from the incident that I had with the student. I'm not sure how the media got ahold of the news so quickly, but as I was being escorted out the building by the security guards and the police, there were local news media outside of the school ready to get information about the incident that would later go viral on social media.

But here is where I became confused about our justice system. As the police were taking me away to the local jail, they said they had seen the video via social media. They stated they saw where the student kicked me first and that I was assaulted, but yet they still arrested me. While I was in the booking area, the police officers in the station began to share the video of me. One of the other students in the classroom had recorded the altercation and shared it on social media. They were all laughing, and some commended me for what I did. One of the officers even let me have some McDonalds before they put me in my jail cell for lock-up. I remember having the cell to myself and sitting there in my thoughts wondering when I was going to get out and what was going to happen to me. Soon a black man approached my cell and told me that I needed to be taken out to speak with an investigator.

Do you remember the scene from the movie *Menace II Society* when the black investigator was talking to the character played by Tyrin Turner

(Caine), and he said that famous line from the movie? "You know you done fucked up, right?"

As that investigator was staring me in my face, this is exactly how I was feeling. It was at that moment that I realized that things weren't going to go in my favor. The next morning I was relieved of my cell and placed in a county van to go to the local county jail. I remember riding in that van with a fluttering heartbeat with two other black men. I felt like I was dreaming because I couldn't believe what the prior day lead up to. Once we arrived at the county jail, the officers lead us to a holding area where we would get processed and booked until we were able to bond out or go to our court date.

I remember while in the holding area we were all waiting to see a doctor. One by one, we all would get our health status before going to our cells that we would call home for the duration of our jail time. I remember telling the doctor that I suffered from high cholesterol.

To avoid a civil lawsuit against the county jail, they rushed me off to the hospital to get a full exam of my health before they sent me back to the jail to sit and wait for the outcome of my freedom. I remembered being shackled hand and foot as if I was a slave on my way to a slave ship just to go to the hospital. I asked the guard if the shackles were necessary, and he told me that all inmates had to endure this when leaving the jail for outside treatment and that he was just doing his job.

It was beyond humiliating, and all I wanted was for it to be over with. When I got to the hospital, one of the guards was gracious enough and allowed me to call my brother to let him know what was happening. After being examined by the doctor, he declared me in good health, and then I was escorted back to jail. Once back at the jail, I was commanded to take my clothes off in exchange for an orange jumpsuit and a faded pair of green drawers. The whole experience was mortifying. The guards didn't care if I were innocent or guilty, all they knew was that I was considered an inmate and they had a job to do to ensure that I didn't break free from incarceration. Just thinking about that orange jumpsuit I get nightmares.

I was housed to a cell alone, and I remember sitting there for thirteen hours. It was sickening, and the isolation of those four walls was driving me insane. The sink was connected to the toilet, and my bed was a steel plate with a thin mattress that I was forced to sleep on. The mattress bedding was a thin, t-shirt like material, and the pillow was barely filled with stuffing. Everything you see on television when it came to prison life was exactly like that in real life, maybe even worse. And it takes the inmates no time to be nosy and ask you *what you're in for?*

I remember one younger inmate had asked me what I was in for, and I lied and said it was for drugs. I'm not sure why I did it, but it was the first thing that rolled off my tongue. Then there was an older OG (original gangsta) that was in there, and he asked me the same thing. Out of respect, I told him the truth. He empathized with me, understanding that I had to do what I had to do. Being in jail is an experience you'll never forget. The mental anguish that inmates go through will have you praying to whatever god you believe in to make your stay swift and make you vow never to do anything else again that could land you in there. I remember on the first night I was there; all night, an inmate was yelling, asking to be let out of his cell. I'm not sure what was exactly wrong with him, but from the terror in his voice, I was hoping that they obliged to his request. It was bone-chilling each time he yelled out.

I remember waking up that Friday morning and the news had spread throughout the jail that Prince had passed away, it was some distracting news for a moment that helped me take my mind off of what I was going through. After some time, I recall the guards coming to my cell to take me down to transportation so that I can go to my court hearing that morning. I remember being in the twilight zone because I was unsure of what would happen at court that morning. As I entered the courtroom, all I remember seeing was the judge and the news media. I was incoherent as I remember just answering "yes" to the questions the judge was asking me.

My then-girlfriend had retained a lawyer to represent me. I hadn't met the lawyer until I entered the courtroom that day. I can't remember much; all I knew is that he spoke on my behalf, and the judge agreed to let me out of jail. However, the release processing took so long. I still had to return back to the jail but was able to put back on my regular clothing I was booked in and wait for them to process me out. That was the longest wait of my life, as I wasn't released until 11:30pm that evening. As I was going through the last processing procedure, one of the cops told me that my case should be cut and dry. They informed me that the juvenile had a long rap sheet, and everything should go in my favor.

As I was leaving out to the jail, I remember being hounded by media. For a moment, I understood what celebrities go through when they are stalked by the paparazzi. But I didn't feel special or elite. I felt like my privacy was being invaded. There was a cameraman with a camera smacked dead in my face and his anchor person walking beside him. However, he was unable to fully get an interview because the cameraman's camera wasn't on, and I was in no mood to be interviewed. I declined to answer any questions they asked me and kept walking toward where my girlfriend was waiting for me.

When we finally made it to my home, I apologized to my girlfriend for her having to endure all that she endured so far. My mind was a bit messed up from the three days in jail, which I didn't feel were rightfully deserved. I took my clothes off and threw them in the garbage. The clothing reminded me of a day that would forever change my life, and I didn't want to see those clothes anymore. I felt violated, and I felt dirty. I ran a hot bath, poured a drink, lit a cigar, and soaked in the tub until I felt normal again. After the bath, I remember speaking to some of my cousins who were checking in on me to see how I was doing. And then I was pressured with the thoughts of how I was going to come up with funds to pay the lawyer. The lawyer who agreed to take my case had a fee of seven grand. I had to borrow money from some of my friends and an uncle. Because the case was so heavy in the media, it was surprising to me that some of my family didn't want to associate themselves with me. It was like I was double punished.

Because of the nature of the case, I was forced to check-in with a probation officer and take a drug test every few weeks. That pissed me off because I couldn't believe I was treated like the criminal when it was the juvenile who evoked the entire ordeal. Because I wasn't a drug user I passed the screening every time I was forced to take a test.

The case began to weigh very heavy on me, and I started to see a therapist to help me deal with the stress of it all. I was out of work, was unable to gain employment while the case was going on, and felt like I didn't have many people in my corner. The media was hounding me, and it was very hard to focus.

After speaking to my lawyer and digging into the case, more things began to unravel about what was going on with the case. There was a lady who happened to be standing at the bus stop the Tuesday after I had told the assistant principal about the students who were running from the school. She reached out to my lawyer and me to tell us that she remember some children talking about how they were going to set me up to get fired. She said she remembers one of the students saying my last name, Pennix. She said she didn't think anything of it until it was all over the news, and she knew she had to say something. I was gracious to her for getting in contact with us. I hired a private investigator to make sure the story was true, and sure enough, it all panned out. I wasn't sure how much this was going to help my case, but I had to try something. My livelihood was at stake, and I needed to clear my name.

By this point, I was in a deep depression. I didn't care if I lived or died. I was in so much mental distress I didn't know if I was coming or going. My girlfriend did as much as she could, but after a while, all of the drama became a bit much for her. By the time my girlfriend had left, I'd seen four therapists. It felt like no one would be able to help me. I just wanted it all to go away, but I had a long road ahead of me.

During the preliminary hearing of the case, I remember the media were looking for me in the courtroom. I was able to blend into the background. By this time, I had cut my beard and was a bit unrecognizable to the media. I was happy about that at the time because that meant a little less harassment until I was to appear before the judge. As I was sitting there waiting for my case to be called, I remember how my girlfriend used to encourage me and told me to lift my head up and smile and go to a happy place. She didn't want the media and others to capture me looking defeated but wanted me to remain uplifted.

As the judge for my case entered into the courtroom from the judge's chambers, I was happy to see a black face staring back at me. After looking over the case documents, the judge granted my lawyer and me a continuance for more time to

26

prepare the case. While a continuance was needed, I was still infuriated with the entire process. My parole officer was waiting outside the courtroom to escort me to another room so that I can take a drug screening drop. I was so insulted because with all the evidence I knew about the juvenile, I was going through what he should have been going through for attempting to set me up. At this point, I felt like he was successful in his plan. My life was ruined while he was probably out terrorizing other people and gloating about what he had done to me.

To help myself earn a living, I decided to enroll in a truck driving school. Because of my record, it was hard getting interviews and hired for any other work. With a pending court case, driving trucks was the best I could do. In between training and school, I continued to see a therapist when I could, but I don't think it was helping much.

Finally, my court continuance date came around July 6, 2016. There were a few cases before mine before I would go before the judge again. Because my lawyer and I had been working on this case and thought that we had some good evidence to show that I was defending myself, I would soon be proved wrong. The justice system is not designed for justice at all. I stood and walked to the defendant's side of the courtroom. I began to give my account of the incident on April 20, 2016. The judge listened to my story, but it would soon mean nothing.

Because I was caught on camera physically assaulting the teen things were not ever going to go in my favor, no matter what the teen's criminal background was. It seemed as if they got two niggas for the price of one. One young black male and one old black male. After conferring with my lawyer, I decided to plea out of the case. I didn't want a felony on my record, which was what was going to happen if I took the case to trial and lost. So to avoid prison time and a felony on my record, I pleaded no contest to a misdemeanor charge of battery. The district attorney on the case didn't care what happened, as long as he has a win on his record, and another black man has a charge on his background. This is how I truly felt about it.

I was so mentally and emotionally drained. I just wanted to go on with my life and leave it all behind me. I'd soon realize that my side of the story was not important. It wasn't important that the juvenile spit on me, nor important that he kicked me, nor important that the entire ordeal was premediated by the juvenile. All that was in important, in my opinion, was can we take another black male down. The court succeeded.

Chapter 2

Because of my ordeal, I realize that our justice system is a continuous cycle of determent to our young black male youths. Black males that are in the system are chewed and spat out. In my opinion, white America views young black males as thugs, and they've become an endangered species that America will be happy if they become extinct. I believe some of the white people that work for the system don't give a fuck about young black males. They won't fight for injustices happening to them, nor black males as a whole. I believe there's some type of enjoyment they get out of locking up black men.

It is big business to incarcerate black lives. Black lives don't mean anything to them. Basically, what the system does is take the misguided, troubled black teenagers and slap them on the wrist throughout their adolescent years. The system sits back and watches them go down the wrong road until they're of legal age, and then slams them with mass incarceration. They allow the young black male to run wild only to lock them up like caged animals. Make money off them with free labor and enslave them to the system.

Unfortunately, I was now a part of this broken system, but I was determined to start my life over. By this time, I'd now completed truck driving school and began my training with over-the-road driving of big rigs. It was helpful in allowing me to clear my mind.

I remember the times of traveling from state to state, myself and the open road. From Seattle, WA to Portland, OR. From Texas to California, clearing my mind, sorting my life out to move forward with the rest of the years I had on this earth.

But it would be a long road to recovery. I did experience a bit of post-traumatic symptoms while on the road at times. When I would go through the mountain in Arizona at times, it would remind me of being locked up in the cell, and it would be hard for me to make it through the mountains. There was a heightened level of paranoia that I experienced when I would be out with my friends — always looking over my shoulder, wondering if I'd have to defend myself or wondering if the juvenile would somehow find me for round two.

Also, my ex-girlfriend and I attempted to work through the relationship, but at the time, I couldn't meet her emotionally where she needed me. She also didn't have the empathetic capacity to meet me where I was at. I'd just come from facing possible six years of my life behind bars for some juvenile who had previously had fifteen different arrests, and she wanted me to put it all behind me like it never happened. I just wasn't able to do that so easily. However, months of on the road driving and seeing a therapist when I would come back home helped me to push past the pain. Unfortunately, my relationship wouldn't survive.

When you're involved in a high-profile case of a small community, it's not so easy to put things behind you, even if you wanted to. I could be at local restaurants minding my business, and locals would walk up me asking me if they knew me. Most of the time, I would say no just to avoid bringing up the incident and reliving it. Some people would stare at me strangely, not being able to remind themselves how they knew my face, while others would immediately recognize me from the news story. I remember one man I ran into actually commended me for what I did by saying, "you had to do what you had to do."

Soon after, I would realize that over-the-road truck driving wasn't going to work, mainly because driving through the mountains. Something about those mountains gave me terrible anxiety, and it would cause me to lose a lot of money on some of my trips. I settled in California for a few weeks to be with family but then would always find my way back to Milwaukee, the town where I had the run-in with the juvenile. Out of work and not willing to deal with the memories that Milwaukee had to offer, I decided to go back home to Chicago. As I journeyed back to Chicago, I lived with my mother for some time to figure out the rest of my life. It felt great to be back home in *Chi-City*, as I called it.

But I knew I needed to stay productive, so I enrolled in a barber college refresher course to renew my professional license. One of my good friends, Mr. D., owned a popular barber college called Chapz Barber School. He supported me in my endeavor, and during the transition in my life, we formed a closer, true friendship and bond for life. He was my instructor and mentor – even played a father-like role in my life during this time. There would be so many times where we would sit down to lunch, and he would give me positive advice on life and encourage me to stay on a righteous path. He drilled in my head about staying away from negative interruptions that would cause me to be detoured from the path that was meant for me. Mr. D's sister, who I call *Auntie*, also became one of my life confidants. She would advise me on situation after situation and proved to be a much-needed staple in my life. They both helped me weather the storms, and I'm grateful that they have crossed my pathway.

Down the way, I met a good old-school Christian man by the name of Roy through Mr. D. Roy is the owner of a barbershop he named after himself, Roy's Barber Shop. Roy allowed me to be employed at his barbershop and also has been another influencer on my life. They encouraged me to attend church and develop a closer relationship with God. Doing this has helped tremendously with what I've gone through in the past few years of my life.

Part of why I'm writing this book is to help those understand that once you've been in a situation like I have, you have to want to improve yourself constantly. With a criminal background, life is not always going to be kind to you. I've done many things like enroll in acting class and taken different jobs always to help myself move forward. But life will continue to test you.

Prior to working at Roy's Barber Shop, I worked with another barber owner who, in so many words, accused me of stealing money by not giving an account for all my clients that I serviced each day. I had to leave that shop because he was coming against my integrity. In this society, it doesn't matter how innocent you believe you are; once you have a background, there will be people who will hold that over your head and challenge your character.

And you always have to be careful of the people you allow in your life. There was a time when I was working at a particular barbershop and I was dating this young lady. She took a liking to me, and we decided to hang out one night. Because I had been dealing with some depressive issues, I was prescribed some anti-depressive medication by my therapist. I call them "happy pills" because their upper effects would cause me to be in a slight state of euphoria.

One day we were hanging out on her birthday, and I happened to have a drink with her while on the medication. It took me a little bit out of my mind. I remember we got into a slight argument to which I gave a slight muff in her forehead. The next thing I know, she'd pulled a knife out on me and chased me out of her apartment.

For me, everything leads me back to April 20, 2016. Had I not had that incident I wouldn't be dealing with depression, I wouldn't have to take anti-depressants, I wouldn't have been in the incident with the woman with the knife. Two things could have happened: she could have killed me, or she could have called the police on me. Although I was here in Chicago, if they would have done a multi-state background check on me and saw the charges from

Milwaukee, my life could be in another uproar right now. When you have a background, the line you walk on as a black man gets thinner. You can't afford to misstep on that rope.

With this newfound understanding of my life, I find myself reading more about the plight of blacks in America. I've read *The New Jim Crow: Mass Incarceration in the Age of Colorblindness* by Michelle Alexander, and I've also watched the Netflix original *13th* produced by Ava Duvernay. Reading and watching these documentarian projects makes my experience even more real and relatable. Because I've been through the system and still feeling the effects of the system, I've become a pseudo-advocate for more projects like these.

41

Even watching documentaries like *I Am Not Your Negro* about a letter written by James Baldwin helped me to learn some frightening things about America's sense of reality when it comes to the black man. White America doesn't always provide the best or a lot of resources to allow us to have the best opportunities. We are cruelly trapped between what we would like to be and what we arc – to America. We cannot possibly become what we would like to because of the emptiness we have. I feel that we're treated to be tamed and seen as ugly. Our story is not pretty, and even in the new millennium, we're still struggling to matter in this world.

In the story of *The Negro in America* by Arnold Rose, it is a hard story to tell and read for that matter. It appears that not everything that is faced can be changed when it comes to black issues. But the oxymoron to it is that nothing can be changed until it has been faced. Unfortunately black, or the Negro's, history is not the past. It is the present. We carry our history with us. I'm encouraged by what the author said that "we are our history." If we pretend otherwise, we literally are criminals.

As James Baldwin recounts in his great speech on civil rights: "A journey is called a journey because you cannot know what you will discover on the journey. You'll never know exactly what you will do with what you find or what it will do to you. And depending upon what you find can weaken yourself in how you deal with the world, as it is, and ourselves as we are. It is not a racial problem. It's a problem of whether you're willing to look at your life and be responsible for it, and then be willing to change it. That great western house I come from is one house and I am one of the children of that house. It is because the American people are unable to face the fact t that I am flesh of their flesh, bone of their bone, created by them. My blood, my father's blood, is in soil."

Chapter 3

But in a side-bar, black America is not just America's problem; white America is America's problem as well. Here are a few of America's problems: school and college shootings

There should be more of an attempt to get down to the roots of such attacks and take up measures to prevent such horrific ordeals in the future. Some incidents always leave us thinking, *why them?* Why those poor children? These mass murders are the worst, and especially when they involve children. Here is a list of some of the worst school massacres.

Sandy Hook Elementary School Massacre, 32 killed.

On December 14, 2012 when Adam Lanza opened fire in Sandy Hook Elementary School in Newton, Connecticut, USA, killing twenty-six children and six adult staff members, it was just one of the many tragic and deadliest school massacres the world has seen, especially in the United States. Violence in schools is a vile and deplorable act, not only because it involves the murder of innocent children but destroys the whole notion of the school being a safe place for a child. School shootings might be rare, but they are extremely tragic and raise several questions about the safety of children. The world has seen some of the most brutal and horrific school shootings and two out of three school massacres have taken place in the last 15 years.

Columbine High School Massacre, 13 dead.

On April 20, 1999 two students Eric Harris and Dylan Keloid murdered twelve students and a teacher at columbine high school in Littleton, Colorado. The pair had also planned a fire bomb to divert fire fighters, 99 explosive devices and bombs rigged in cars. They also injured twenty-four other students and the two later committed suicides in the school library. This school massacre is one of the deadliest school shootings whilst in a high school campus in America and sparked several debates about gun control, bullying and violent video games.

In recent years, it has emerged that the pair had meticulously planned their suicide in a poorly implemented terrorist bombing and had never been victims of bullying but were in fact bullying other students.

Virginia Tech Shooting, at least 31 people killed.

At least thirty- three people were killed on a Monday on the campus of Virginia Tech in what appears to be the deadliest shooting rampage in American history. Many of the victims were students shot in a dorm and a classroom building. The university was struck with a tragedy that we consider of monumental proportions, said this evening that is 15 people were wounded by the gunman, although there were other reports of higher numbers of injuries. Witnesses described scenes of mass chaos and unimaginable horror as some students were lined up against a wall and shot. Others jumped out of windows to escape or crouched on floors to take cover. The killings occurred in two separate attacks on that campus in Blacksburg, VA. The first took place around 7:15am. When two people were shot and killed at the dormitory. There was more than two and half hours later, thirty-one others, including the gunman, were shot and killed across campus in a classroom building, where some of the doors had been chained. Victims were found in different locations around the building. The first attack started as students were getting ready for classes or were on their way there. The university did not evacuate the campus or notify students of that attack until several hours later.

University of Texas Massacre, 16 killed.

On August 1, 1966, after stabbing his mother and his wife to death the night before Charles Whitman, a former marine, took riffles and other weapons to the observation desk atop minutes he shot and killed 16 people including one unborn child, and injured 31 others, while a final victim died in 2001 from the lingering effects of his wounds. The incident ended when a policeman and a civilian reached Whitman and shot him dead. The attack is one of the deadliest mass shootings in U.S. history. Charles Whitman, 25 was studying architectural engineering. In 1961 Whitman was admitted to the University of

Texas at Austin on a scholarship from the naval enlisted science education program. While at University of Texas, Whitman met and married his wife, Kathleen. Whitman struggled with gambling and bad grades, and he lost his scholarship in 1963. Before the attack, Whitman had sought professional help for 'overwhelming violent impulses.' Also including fantasies about shooting people from the tower. An autopsy after his death revealed a brain tumor.

Parkland Florida High School Shootings, 17 killed.

A teen gunman accused of opening fire with a semi-automatic rifle at his former high school in Parkland, Florida has been charged with 17 counts of premeditated murder, officials said. The authorities said the suspect, identified as 19-year-old Nikolas Cruz, concealed himself in the crowd fleeing Marjory Stone Douglas High School following the massacre on Wednesday afternoon. He was arrested in nearby Coral Springs. Fourteen others were wounded, five with life- threatening injuries, hospital officials said. Cruz had recently been expelled from Douglas for disciplinary reasons and was enrolled elsewhere in the district, the school's superintendent in board county, Robert Runcie, said. Cruz took an uber to the Douglas campus on Wednesday, Runcie told nbc news. The gunman was believed to have been armed with an ar 15 style semi- automatic rifle and multiple magazines, said board county sheriff Scott Israel. It was unclear whether he had any other weapons, Israel said. There was no indication that the gunman had an accomplice or accomplices, federal and local authorities said.

Chapter 4

When I read Charlemagne Tha God's book, *Black Privilege,* it encouraged me to live more in my truth as he told more about his truth. It encouraged me to follow more after the passions of life that empowered me and lifted me up.

Through my journey after the incident with the juvenile, I took some acting classes to pursue one of my passions in life. It was something I was just trying to see what would happen. When your life is almost taken away from you, there is something in you that gives you the nerve to just go for anything. I was happy to land a small role in the drama series *Empire.* It was an experience of a lifetime. I wasn't an extra, but an actual actor and was paid for my services. I recount the day, and I was high in my spirits. We were given our location to meet for the shuttle bus to drive us to set. I remember parking my car in the actor's lot and getting on that bus thinking I was on my way to Hollywood.

When I got to set, I recall being in a room of about 200 actors at the time. I wasn't expecting to see that many people, but nevertheless, I was determined. The casting director picked me out of all the actors that were there to be on the show. I was so excited to be chosen to be in a scene with the main characters of the show. I remember meeting Jussie Smollett, I was cool and told him my name, and that I thought his music was cool and that I was a fan. It was a memorable day because I remember it being my granddad's birthday, January 21st. It felt like a good luck day for me because it had been a long time since something really good had happened in my life.

As I was talking to Jussie, I was telling him how I had recently watched the Thurgood Marshall story the year before, and I saw him in the movie. Then I was amazed that the next year I'm on the TV show with him, and I'm meeting him. He told me that was God's doing – and I believe it. It's funny because I was chosen a second time as a cast member of *Empire,* and this time it was my grandmother's birthday, February 22nd. This particular time I was able to meet the entire cast of the show and also Forest Whitaker and Alfre Woodard.

As a young black boy who grew up on the Southside of Chicago straight out of the projects to

56

being on a hit television show with mega stars. For me, this was a great accomplishment thus far. I was still being determined about turning my life around despite the misfortune that happened to me in my life just a few years earlier.

But my time as an actor was short-lived. Although I haven't quit acting, the roles stopped coming, and life was back to reality. Did mention I don't trust lawyers? I empathize with the likes of Pac, Puffy, Jay-Z, and every other black man that has gone through the system or any oppressive experience in life. You will always have the haters and suckers trying to get in your way to try to stop you from living your dreams. I don't trust lawyers because they play with your life once you get into the system. I strongly suggest that you arrange an immediate face-to-face meeting with your attorney to discuss all your concerns upon retaining them.

Great communication is essential in the client-attorney relationship. The reason I bring this up in this part of my story is that as I personally began to dig into my case, I realized that I was just another client to my attorney. There was not a great deal of care taken for me in my case. Trust is the most important part of your relationship with your lawyer. My lawyer didn't keep me informed about important information pertaining to my case. When calling him, I'd get blown off and disregarded. I don't believe that is how I was supposed to be treated.

I feel sorry for the young black race; young black men don't have a fighting chance. Combining rap music and the drugs, the young generation is continually a target for this society to further put them into ruins. After watching *13ᵗʰ* on Netflix, I continue to see how the justice system banks on young blacks to not be able to afford good lawyers to plead their cases properly. The system also knows that a young black male will take a plea bargain quicker than they're willing to allow their case to go to trial.

After spending time in Wisconsin, I realize that it's not a place for black people to live. After my case was over, I did some research about the state of Wisconsin and was ashamed about the statistics on several fronts pointing towards glaring clarity of how it is for black people living in the state. At the time of research, Wisconsin had the worst record in the nation for teaching black students to read.

Surprisingly they were worse than Alabama and Mississippi, and they have the widest gap of any state in the union between black and white students.

In the city of Milwaukee, where I taught, they test the student four times a year in reading and math in the fourth grade, and then they assess the reading and math levels again in the eighth grades. It's found that in the eighth-grade reading and math have the largest gaps between the white and black students. It is also reported that Wisconsin puts more black men in prison than all the other states; Oklahoma is second. It is said that one out of every eight black men in Wisconsin is incarcerated. I don't think any of these statistics are all that surprising to those of us who have lived in the state as a black person. if you are black living in Wisconsin, it's a living hell.

I believe part of the problem is that they don't have enough people willing to speak up for themselves. Speak up for their community and for the overall quality of life for those living in Milwaukee. A few years ago, *the school choice program* was introduced and hailed as the magic bullet to improve education. But this hasn't been proven to make it any better, because there are students who can afford to go to private schools and families will send their children to schools who only had the best achievement rates – and the rest of the students spilled over to low performing schools. But it still goes to show, based on academia testing, that the school systems in Wisconsin are still failing to properly educate black students.

I wish we lived in a perfect world. I wish there was a perfect world where there were no crimes, no school shootings, no pipeline to prison system. But let's be real, who are we fooling? This is not a perfect world; it's a cold world. I always recount my incident in my head and wonder what I could have done differently. Always questioning God why did it have to happen to me? I've resolved to say in my mind that God has his picks or his favorites, and we all must be put through tests.

I guess I lacked some sort of faith, and God wanted to strengthen mine. Maybe I needed more belief in him, to gain a stronger, better relationship with him in my heart. Maybe this is the story for many other young black people who have been routinely mischaracterized in the news, or television shows, and in everyday conversations. Labeled as thugs or being label as unintelligent children. Maybe God wants us to just call on his name more. I have no idea what it is, but I wish it would stop.

I wish I knew why there is black-on-black violence, and why we can't see how we're hurting each other. Every ghetto in the United States is plagued by forces from the inside as well as the outside. We're fighting two enemies that we can't seem to get the advantage over. The behavior of young black Americans with little concern about their attitudes, ideas, wants, and desires have brought them down to a low estate that they can't seem to pull themselves out of. The lack of educational and employment opportunities, prison reform, and racism in America, leaves little to the black youth perspectives to desire. They recognize that they are rarely included as a part of strategies of framing solutions to problems that directly impact them. All I can say to young black brothers is to keep your head up as would Pac say.

Chapter 5

Don't be afraid to seek help from a therapist. We know in the black community we are shunned if we choose to see a therapist, but many of us suffer in silence because we hold a lot of our negative thoughts inside. We don't know how to pray, so have no one who we can actually vent our hurts and pains to.

I made that important judgment call on my life because there was a time I had troubling thoughts, feelings, or moods, and it scared me. Are you feeling overwhelmed or unlike yourself? Do you ever think it would help you if you had someone to talk to? Someone like a therapist?

We can't be afraid of letting go of old fashioned stigmas. Holding on to these outdated ideologies deter us from getting the mental health care that we need. No problem is too big or too small. If it's bothering you enough to where it's affecting your everyday life, then it's worth speaking to a mental health professional about it. Seeking therapy doesn't mean that you're crazy or insane; it means you recognize that there is something that is troubling you that you want to get ahead of before it turns worse.

For me, I wanted to turn my life around and *live my best life,* as Snoop Dog would say. I owed it to myself to go out there in the world and make a better life for myself, and so do you. Once you've been in the type of situation that I have been in you have two choices: either lie down and die or pick yourself up and keep living. I chose to keep living.

There were a lot of people in my corner who looked out for me financially during my case. So I had to work against some major odds just to pay them back the money that was lent to me from friends and family. During this time, I was able to see who my real friends and family were. Because I'm a hip-hop fan, all I could think about was how Tupac might have felt when he got out of jail. He was on a mission to get his life back on track. He had lost a lot of time due to the unfortunate circumstance he was in. I was faced with the same boat. Three days in jail, a loss of employment, and a conviction on my record. People who I thought were going to be there for me weren't, and at that moment I understood that when the world or people turn their backs on you, you must keep on keeping on.

That is what life is about. You're going to have some ups and downs in this life – but the downs should never stop you from moving. If you never go through anything, how will you know what you're made of? In this life, you got to take the bitter with the sweet. Not meaning to be cliché, but those adages weren't said for no reason. Someone went through something horrific, and through the wisdom they gained from learning the lessons, they were able to pass down encouraging quotes that will live throughout the ages. I can only hope that my story can produce some of the same inspiring messages.

During my trial, I understood how jail had become a big business. As I said before, during my situation, I remembered a lot of what Tupac had said in interviews he did during and after his incarcerations prior to his death. I remember Pac saying that the prison system was selling spaces in jail because they were feeding the small towns and giving the communities jobs. While I'm all for building the local communities, this jail system seems to be at the expense of young black males. You read about this in books and watch the revelations in documentaries, but you never really understand it in its full capacity until you're actually living through it.

I remember when I was doing interviews regarding the case and my situation. I remember my sole purpose in doing the interviews was to tell my side of the story. I knew I had to be careful about the interviews I did because of the way the media can spend a narrative in the way that they feel would be more entertaining. I recall doing an interview with major outlets like CBS News, FOX News, and ABC News. When the reporters would ask me what I wanted to get out of doing the interview, I would mainly say, "Please just paint me in the best light possible." I've said that countless times. I didn't want to be demonized or criminalized no more than I had already been.

After the case was over, I remember that the reporters were all waiting for me to give an official statement about how I felt. But I took control of my narrative at that time and told them that I would speak to the media at a later date. I wanted to be in control of the setting. I didn't want to just speak in the space of raw emotion. I wanted to have time to think about what I wanted to say and articulate myself in the best way possible.

Chapter 6

Everything happens for a reason, and I know God saw my life's journey from the day I came out of my mother's womb. Because I lost my career in education, I was forced to learn other trades to make a living for myself. Some of my bigger life lessons I'd learn are from being a truck driver and dealing with unfavorable people.

I remember working for this bus company. I relocated to Green Bay, Wisconsin, because I wanted to learn how to drive coach buses. The company had given me a company vehicle to use during my stay in Green Bay, and I was staying in a hotel for a few days. While I was already used to dealing with some level of racism from being in Milwaukee, I received a bit more of a taste of it while in Green Bay.

I was dealing with some real red-neck, white folks, and I was the only black man in the entire training. I recall them finding out that I was from Milwaukee, so they nicked-name me Milwaukee the entire time that I was there. They also gave me the side-eye the entire time, too. Green Bay folks had a stigma about black folks from Milwaukee. They assumed that we were all no good and that we'd cause trouble in their city. Given what I had already been through, I was just hoping that that part of my background didn't come up to avoid further humiliation from those white men.

I remember during my time in Green Bay, the Colin Kaepernick issue was really big in the news, and he was facing controversy because he was taking a knee against racism. My trainer was this older white man, and he asked me about my opinion on Kaepernick. Let's just say I wasn't thinking quickly on my feet. Lord only knows why I allowed him to set me up for the Okie-Doke, but I gave my opinion, and it went downhill from there. I told him that Kaepernick had a right to stand up for what he believed in and that no one should interfere with that. The white trainer was taken aback by my statement and the next thing I knew, I didn't get the job after the training.

I laugh about it now, because I've had the pleasure of having my CDL license for 13 years now, but at the time I was crushed. It bothered me that this man had the power to take away a job I deserved all because of my opinion. But that's the world we live in today.

When I originally decided to try my experience in the classroom, I did it with the mindset that I would be helping form and change young minds. However, that wasn't my experience. I felt like a damn babysitter most of the time. While some kids were cool, most of them had a lot of problems. Many of them came to school just to make sure they got a meal for the day. Some of them came to school to escape what they were going through at home. When I think about what I face as a grown man and how sometimes it's hard for me to maintain my sanity just dealing with adult issues, I can just imagine what some of these children were dealing with.

These children were facing some major emotional and anger issues, and it was evident from the countless fights that I had to break up while teaching. I recount one time that a fight between students was so bad that when I went to help security break up a fight, I ended up with a sprained ankle. One security guard even told me that he doesn't even put much effort into breaking up student fights because the school board doesn't pay worker's compensation in the event they get hurt. This was a sad notion to me because it was as if no one cared but me. Many of my colleagues would opt out of the classroom for the sake of mental and physical health because the classroom could really put wear and tear on the mind and physical body.

While the school incident was still getting captured in the news, I remember going to the NFL Draft in Chicago. Because my face had been all over the news during the trial, I was sure that people would recognize me. I was afraid that people would want to talk to me about the incident or that I was going to have some adversarial people coming against me for what I did to the juvenile. But I loved football and had never had the opportunity to go to an NFL draft event before, so I pressed through and didn't allow the paranoia to overcome me. I'm bringing this up because you just never know how a small incident can affect your entire life and then add on media coverage to it, and it changes your perception of the world around you indefinitely.

You have to understand the pressure a black man is under when he's fighting for his life. Even when going to court, you're fighting for your life even just by the way you dress. I remember my cousin told me always to make sure that I was well dressed for court. He told me the white man was already analyzing me, and I couldn't let him think that I was a thug or deserved the jail time that I was facing because of the way that I looked. That jewel of knowledge helped with me, and every time I went to court, I was always aware of my attire.

Apart from my therapy, there were many things that kept my spirit uplifted. I pulled inspiration from any place that I could that would help me keep moving forward in my life. I was inspired by the 2018 movie *Black Panther*. Seeing this movie reminded me to stand up and be a king. By this time I was going through my civil suit against the Milwaukee School Board because I felt that I was wrongly terminated. Seeing *Black Panther* helped me to continue to fight for myself. The Wakandians had something to live and stand for, and I felt I did too. I left the movie with a sense of pride, knowing that there was nothing too large for me to conquer.

I even pulled on the spirit of Muhammad Ali. On one trip that I had to take to Louisville, KY, I remember that was the birthplace of Ali. As I was traveling through the city and thinking about all that I was going through I remember about his fight to the top. Nothing stopped him from believing in himself. During the layover that I had in Louisville, I ended up staying at a hotel that was located in the hood of the city. It was a lot going on, and I took in the scene to remind myself that I have more to live than what the past experience with the juvenile was trying to reduce me to. It was as if Ali's spirit began to flow through me and began to encourage me to say that I won't be reduced to just some man in the system, but I'll overcome this and do greater.

But also there are other things that need to be addressed as well if we're going to be honest and man up. We have to stop the black on black crime we do to ourselves within our communities. We allow the system to pit us against each other and be crabs in a bucket. We say we want a revolution but can't form together in unity to even get it started. The first step for change is accountability. If we don't force ourselves to be accountable for the detriment that we cause to ourselves, we'll never be able to fight the larger enemy.

Chapter 8

In the Milwaukee Journal Sentinel, it was reported of past school violence within the Milwaukee Public School System. It has reports of an 18-year-old that punched his school's football coach and grabbed the coach's genitals. Then there are reports of two middle-school-age sisters that jumped a police officer who was called to calm a disturbance that was involving the two sisters. Then a grandmother who charged a group of students at an elementary school and then struck the principal.

While violence in public schools is not limited to Milwaukee, as we know of violence that has happened in Chicago and other high-crime metropolitan cities, we have to wonder how we stop it and bring about solutions to this problem. We all know of major school budget cuts, and the students aren't receiving the proper education needed to shape their minds in a more productive manner. But the students aren't the only individuals who are suffering from these poor educational environments; the staff suffers as well.

If you search my name in Google, I'm sure you'll find the horrific incident between myself and the student that went viral on social media. But there is a lot that the video didn't tell about the story. The narrative that the video shows is of an upset black man taking a juvenile teenager down to the floor. But if you look more closely, you'll see a disrespectful teen that was hardheaded and didn't want to listen nor had any respect for authority. In no way was I trying to show I was crazy or radical. I had just encountered a wild teen who wouldn't back down when asking him to behave himself. It was just me against a student, with other students further instigating and antagonizing the situation. There also was another teacher in the room who just stood by afraid to do anything. I felt like I was on an island alone, with a bunch of teens ganging up against me. My attempt to diffuse the situation didn't exactly go as planned, but many don't understand how I felt in danger of my life. I'm no stranger to how violent the children can get, and when you have someone in your face not willing to back down, you do what you only know to do, and that's to fight back. Although I was dealing with a teenager, I was dealing with a teenager who thought he was a man. A teenager who felt he had something to prove. A teenager who thought he could go toe-to-toe with a grown man. I can't say that in hindsight that I would have done anything differently because of the nature of the situation, but I can say is that I wish it wasn't me that was assigned to substitute that class.

I remember studying Islam at one time when I moved back to Chicago. My old teacher from barber college and friend/brother Earl Mohamed schooled me more about The Nation and things I didn't know about our past as black people. Every Monday, I would go to class and learn about The Nation and Brother Malcolm X. I remember showing Brother Earl the video of me and the juvenile, and I remember him telling me, "Brother, you were off your dean."

This was a term to mean that I was *off my square* or didn't exercise self-control. I respected what Brother Earl was saying to me and took in a lot of what he taught me, but as I look over the situation, I just can't see how I would have been able to avoid the situation. I think not doing anything would have further exacerbated the situation even more, and it probably would have turned out worse than what actually happened.

While I never could see myself fully converting to The Nation of Islam, mainly because I didn't want to conform to the strict lifestyle changes, I appreciated a lot of the teachings that I learned from Brother Earl. You can learn a lot about self-discipline from the Muslim practices, and their teachings teach you a lot about self-awareness and accountability, which we could all benefit from.

We live in a world where there are two societies going on: the black and the white nation. While I know there are other minorities in this country that face racial injustices that plague us as well. I'm speaking specifically to the plight that I, as a black man and other black men, face every day in a white society. We have come far within this world of racial disparity, but we have such a far ways to go. I'm not sure if we'll ever come to a true place of racial equality. It seems like every time we take a leap forward something else comes along to either keep us at a standstill or push us backward.

We're still fighting for unity within our own community as well as fighting for a seat at the table within a world that never truly wanted to include us in the first place. Have you ever wondered why the black man always blames everything *on the man*? Try being an upstanding citizen, trying your best to live a decent life, attempting to ensure you're an upstanding role model, and then have one bad slip of judgment. Suddenly the whole world falls on your shoulders, and you see life in a new picture that you never saw before. Yes, I had some glimpse into the world of injustice, merely based on where I grew up and some other past things I experienced, but nothing like what I experienced after the juvenile incident.

Other songs that speak the words I can't speak about how I feel about life as a black man are

Teardrops and Closed Caskets by Outlawz and 2Pac, and *God Gave Me Style* by 50 Cent. Music has been one of the main go-to therapy options for me. I get lost in lyrics, and I'm able to get my feelings out therapeutically. And that's why our black brothers are so stressed out and full of anger because we hold so much in and don't tell our stories. I'm trying to tell my story as a means to encourage someone that has been in my shoes to tell their story.

There's an old school song called *We're All in the Same Gang* by the West-Coast Rap All-Stars. It's a song that is trying to bridge the gap of unity amongst us. Like we separate ourselves to these different gang affiliations or hoods or parts of town, but when we look at it – we're all in the same gang. Black minorities are trying to release ourselves from the struggle. No one really wants to be in the struggle, but sometimes we feel that it's all we have. Some of us go through what I went through and continue to spiral down to lower states of being, never to fully recover. Then you have others, like me, who keep fighting, even though the fight is killing us because it's causing diseases within our bodies that are stress-induced.

There is a song, *Free* by a group called Goodie Mob that I would listen to in my car all the time. I'd zone out to the song and soak up the message. I would be praying to God to be free, to be delivered from the struggle that I was in. Not wanting to give up but tired of fighting. Then 2Pac would go further into my pain with his song *It Ain't Easy*. This song speaks the words of every black man in America.

The reason I'm telling you all about these songs is because the hip-hop community is often overlooked because it is narrated to be glorifying the ghetto life or gang life or drug life. But if you really listen to some songs, there are actually deep messages in the songs. Songs that the artists are crying out for the world to hear us and understand the plight and detriments that we're going through. We don't want to live these lives, but no one will let us break free from it. It is not just for entertainment purposes – listen intently and try your best to empathize with us as black men.

Chapter 9

While we may look at the children and feel sorry for the upbringing that they've been brought up in, sometimes we have to look at other things that they children may need. Some of them need a good old fashion James Evans ass kicking. We've stopped disciplining our children, and I believe that this is a big part of why many of our children go astray. Some like to argue that child discipline by way of whippings or spankings don't work, but I beg to differ. I grew up in a generation where this was commonplace, and it seemed to steer us in the right direction. Now don't get me wrong, I understand that butt-whippings are not a one-size-fits-all approach, as we do need to use wisdom when disciplining our children. But we know there are many who will agree with me that lack of discipline makes for a rotten child.

Also, our young black children need both parents in their lives. Balance in the home makes for a better upbringing – but both parents need to be emotionally present, not just physically. When I think back on the show *Good Times*, James Evans was a real strong black man with good morals and who wanted the best for his children. He was reserved when needed to be and disciplined when it was needed. Showed to be a good husband to his wife and understood the value of family. While he still experienced the hardships that a lot of black families still experience today, he didn't use that as an excuse to give up on his family. Some of these fathers in today's society need a James Evans ass-kicking, too, if you ask me. As a black community, we've lost a bit of our way. Where are our stern fathers like James Evans? Who cares about our families and our children?

It's important for people to understand how this situation affected me so much. Don't mean to sound like a broken record, but I needed to say so much about my life and story and what it has done to me. I remember at one point I wanted to get on a talk show like *Ellen* or *The Steve Harvey Show* because I felt that if I had a wider audience, then it would make that much more of a difference in pulling the covers off of the treatment of blacks in America, in our justice system, and in the school system. I remember I used to practice on my Mac Book and record myself, practicing as if I was on the talk shows telling my story. Even hoping that the juvenile that I had the incident with, if we can come together and heal within ourselves and resolve the issue, and then see how we can help others.

The truth of the matter, I never wanted what happened to happen, but what's done is done now. And even now it's proven that the young man needed more intervention in his life. He's spent time in the penitentiary for other crimes he had done, and he's continually on this rat race of life. I'm hoping that at some point he will be able to turn his life around. He doesn't deserve to be another statistic within this criminal system that is not meant to protect us, but only to keep us in bondage to ourselves.

I'm on a constant quest to try to understand why black men are so hated in this world. The burning question I'd like to get answered from a white man is: why do you hate us? I once read a study that said white men have a fear of black people. But why? History will show that we're actually not the violent ones – which slavery proves that each and every time we take a peek back and relive and review it. I also remember reading in the Guardian Newspaper once before that most of these white men who fear black people are without proper education. Maybe it's their fear that black people, men particular, who are more educated than white men, will have a better advantage. But theoretically, isn't that the point of having more education? No matter the race, isn't the person who is deemed more educated supposed to be the one who has the advantage? Again, they create a system that is only beneficial to them.

Even when one throws religion into the mix, their fear isn't really tied to a religious belief, but more so to a thought of inferiority, they believe within themselves that they have. They infest our neighborhoods with drugs and guns – then they armed themselves more heavily with guns in order to protect themselves. And when Obama was in office, it didn't make things any better. The white men were afraid that Obama would empower the minorities. Obama rallied for the poor, which included white people. But whites are so blinded by their hatred that they were willing to vote against bills that would benefit them, just to vote against a black man.

The gun culture in America is getting out of control. Because white men fear black people and have a stigma against us when it comes to violence, there is always an emotional response to us by way of killing us when we're unarmed or posed no threat at all. Take the Philando Castile incident. Castile was a law-abiding citizen trying to do the right thing, following the rules. And because of an over-emotional cop who panicked because of whatever stigma he had in his mind concerning black men, he killed an innocent man in front of his daughter and girlfriend. These two people will be forever scarred in their minds.

I'm sick and tired of us being oppressed on every side of the wall. The white man is like Pharaoh, and I'm Moses screaming, *let my people go!* We want to be free. We want a chance to figure things out and survive and have our communities back. An overhaul of the entire system, but I think with that request, I may be asking for too much. But I'm not the only black man who has been screaming and begging for this. When will our voices be heard?

Chapter 10

Sometimes I talk to the OGs in my neighborhood who've been through the system and get advice from them on how to get through the rest of life. Because even though I fight and have the determination not to allow this to beat me, some days, I have doubts and I get weak. Even the flashbacks from being locked up can knock me off my mental stability and get me down for a moment. I believe on some level I have PTSD – things will trigger me, and I'd have to shake it off and get my mind right.

I talk to my friends and some family who've served ten years or more in jail and ask them how they cope. Many of their advice is just to be careful about the things I do going forward. Always be aware of my temper and slow down. After you've been in a situation like mine, you spend a lot of time thinking, and you don't always make sudden decisions like you would in the past. I think about a song by Naughty by Nature called *The Chain Remains*, and it seems like no matter how many years you've been out of the jail system, it can still feel like you're locked up. And the chains are all over society.

We saw this in the 70s, 80s, and 90s how black men were taken out of the homes – either by death or by jail sentences, and the ones that were left grew up without a father being in the home. In the normal society within the black community, the women outnumber the men. In some respect, I believe this has had a psychological effect on our community, but it's as if no one seems to notice. I think about J. Cole's record, *28th*, where he asks, "What's the price of a black man?" Really, what is the price? If you can't empathize with the plight of the black man then you are part of the problem. You'll never understand why it was important for me to tell my story. You'll never understand why I needed you to read over and over all the struggles that I've been through.

Even getting a job is hard, and even if you feel like my sentence was justified, think about men that have been innocently criminalized. There are men out there who have sat in jail innocent of the crimes that have been placed upon them, but because the price of the black man is so high, no one cared or fought for him. A black man and a white man can commit the same crime, and even without pulling the statistical data, I'd bet my last that 75% of the sentencing for the black man was far harsher than for the white man. Time served ruins your life and forces you to have to jump through a lot of hurdles just to sustain yourself.

I remember I applied for a job as a driver for Amazon. On my application, I told them upfront about my conviction. I did an interview and was scheduled for orientation. I'm assuming that because I was honest about my conviction and had a pretty clean record since the incident that everything was fine. The day I was supposed to go to my orientation, I received a call from the Amazon office telling me that because of my background check came back unfavorable that I was unable to be hired with the company. I was so frustrated. Here I am trying to move on with my life, and this one incident keeps on coming up.

This is the dilemma of thousands of men who have been in the criminal system. The point of jail time is supposed to re-institutionalize us, but it doesn't. It keeps us further incriminated, and some choose to resort back to criminal activity just to take care of themselves. When will someone on the other side look at this and actually choose to give a damn? Because from my perspective, no one does. Black people can't pull themselves from this because we aren't the ones that instituted this system.

Life has gotten so stressful for me that I can't even donate blood. With a lot of the stressor that I've been dealing with since the incident, I've had high blood pressure issues. My girlfriend, at the time, convinced me to go and donate some blood with her. So when we were at the blood bank when they took my blood pressure, they said it was too high to donate the blood. So I left the blood bank and decided to go another time. Then on the second time, I attempted to donate blood, I was told that I couldn't donate because I had been to jail. I was told that because of disease and the possibility of being raped while in jail, I would have to wait a year and come back and try again. I couldn't believe it. The smallest things you don't think being incarcerated will hinder, it will.

So as I'm writing this book, I'm trying to put every possible experience I've encountered since going through the ordeal to show how your life can be completely disrupted. I'm hoping that people can look at my life and slow down in their thinking and maybe having a different reaction. I still stand on that I feared my life in the situation with the juvenile, and I'm utterly pissed with the school board for not having my back. I'm the one that should have been protected. I'm the one that they should have had lawyers lined up to help me beat my case. The school board cared about no one but themselves. Not even the juvenile of the incident, because if they did care they would have been trying to help him in some way. The should have cared about him not continuing to going down the criminal road that he was on.

I'm constantly trying to reinvent myself and pushing myself harder and harder. As you've read in early chapters I've renewed my CDL, renewed my barbering license, and even taken some acting classes. I am trying to perfect my craft in acting in hopes of getting a career going. As you know, I've done the show *Empire*, and I've also been blessed to get a few more gigs. I've had a role in the movie called *Beats* with Anthony Anderson, which appeared on Netflix. I have a small role on the show *The Chi*, which airs on Showtime. Another show I appeared in twice called *Red Line*, and a list of so many other shows. Constantly pursuing, no matter how rough the road seems to get.

My goal is to be there for my fellow brothers, wondering who I can help along the way. I think about an old movie called *South Central*. The main character, OG Bobbie Johnson, was locked up in jail with an old running mate of his from the streets.

Somehow Johnson's friend had gotten himself strung out and was struggling in jail with some white gang members. Long story short, while Johnson was trying to help his friend, he ended up needing some help to fend off the white gang in the jail. A Muslim Brother in the jail decided to help Johnson out of his troubles. Johnson wanted to repay him for his deed, and all the Muslim Brother wanted Johnson to do was educate himself. He asked Johnson to read for 2 hours every day. He didn't want Johnson to become a slave to him but wanted Johnson to educate himself.

And I think for me that is what my endeavor with this book is. Let's educate one another and learn to look out for one another. How can we stand in unity? How can we help that troubled teen? How can we not cause the next man to get locked up? How can we help one another make better decisions?

I ask myself every day, was I really needed in that classroom that day? It wasn't a regular day that day, and most of the teens in that class, I'd later find out, had records. Why wasn't there some other alternative? I go over and over about it in my head a lot. I'm thinking about what if I was a scrawny little teacher, or some thin-framed lady teacher or substitute – how would the situation have gone down? Those children were dead set on being bullies, and there was no one there to protect us from them, nor help them protect themselves from themselves. Do we just give up on our children as lost causes, or do we keep fighting for their success no matter how far they have fallen?

Chapter 11

Like it or not, I'm telling my story. I must tell my story because it's my life. I have to reclaim my life back. There was a time when I was really upset and angry about everything that has happened to me. I didn't feel like anyone really understood what I was going through. I felt judged, and I was always on guard, ready to defend myself. I learned to accept my place in this world when it comes to the system and this government, but it doesn't mean I'm going to take the abuse and mistreatment lying down.

If I can help it at all, I don't want anyone to ever go through what I've gone through, especially a black man. The lies and bullshit changed my life forever.

Your lie and bullshit change my life; it really did. The school board swept bad issues under the rug and attempted to make me appear to be the crazy or bad one. All in the news media, I'm perpetuated as this *angry black man who beats up a student*. The media wouldn't even hardly report on the background of the juvenile. I was the scapegoat, the one who was going to be the fall guy, and it hurts. I lost so much due to this incident — relationships, friends, career, money, and so much more. Two lives were lost in this incident: myself and the juvenile. If you Google my name and search, you'll find out what the juvenile has been up to since the incident. No one saved him. No one helped him from further messing up his record. No one reached out to him and said, *let me help you change your life*. While I may be speaking presumptuously with the previous statement, but thinking back, maybe he didn't want any help. Maybe someone was trying to look out for him, and he chose against it?

They turned me into a criminal for a baby crime. Should I really have been given a conviction? Could there have been some other action taken that could have been a better resolution? Because of the mental anguish I've experienced, there were times I felt like suicide was a better answer. Or when I was angry, and I actually did want to hurt someone who deserved it because my life was falling apart, and I couldn't control it. The torment that I went through at times, thinking that things weren't going to get better.

Having to protect myself from myself because, at times, I did feel a bit mentally unstable. Asking my friends to remove knives out of my reach and trying to ignore crazy thoughts going through my head. I even had a flashback from when I was younger being stabbed by a young teenage gangbanger and thinking that I will forever have to defend myself against those that are out to get me.

It takes a lot of mental energy to overcome your fears and push through. Even with truck driving for some reason, those mountains and bridges put me in a state of fear. For a short while, I'd given up on driving trucks because my fear was paralyzing. But I'm happy to say that I most recently overcome my anxiety and fear of bridges and even alligators in a most recent drive to New Orleans, and overcoming the fear was exhilarating. On the way to New Orleans, I was a passenger, and I remember feeling overwhelmed as we went over the long bridges, but as we were leaving I took the driver's seat, and I was determined to overcome. Once I was able to do that, I had a new sense of pride and determination for the rest of my life.

I'm currently in the pursuit of happiness. Sometimes depression still sneaks up on me, and I turn to things that will help me move past it. One of the movies I watch during these times is *The Pursuit of Happyness*. Seeing Will Smith on that screen struggle through some of the most difficult hardships is like a rope that pulls me right out of my depression. At the end, when he finally gets the opportunity that he's been fighting for, and then he thrust his arms up in the air with exhilaration. To overcome homelessness, joblessness, and all the other things coming up against a black man, and knowing that it's based on a real-life story is so encouraging to me. If it can happen to him, then I know it can happen to me!

Then there's Denzel Washington. There are three movies he starred in that always lift me up: *Malcolm X, The Book of Eli,* and *Hurricane.* All three of these movies are about triumph and carrying out the plan specifically for your life. In *Malcolm X,* he emerged from ruins to become one of the most reverence men in the black community. As he began to find himself spiritually, he was determined to enlighten everyone else around him. The way Denzel played the character of Malcolm X made me feel like

119

I was seeing him during the time he was alive. It forces me to look at myself and be the best man I can be in my community.

Then when we get to *The Book of Eli*, the determination of Eli to carry out the will keeps me going. He was sure of himself and was confident in what his purpose was. No matter what, nothing could get him off of his mission, and that's what I'm determined to do. And lastly, in *Hurricane,* how can I not relate to Rubin "Hurricane" Carter? Wrongfully accused but never gave up, and in the end justice prevailed, and he was freed! I believe I will be free from all of this one day. I believe that what I've gone through will not be able to hold me back. While I am free in the physical sense, there are still some mental barriers that I have to overcome, and I strive to overcome them every day.

I'm constantly on a positive journey, and anything that I can read, watch, listen to that will keep me encouraged and uplifted I've been pouring myself into. It's true what they say that what you feed your mind is what will drive you.

Chapter 12

As I conclude this book, I'd like to talk a little bit about my mentor, my friend, my everything, Mr. D. When I met Mr. D., he seemed to be the coolest guy on the planet. I had heard of him prior to officially meeting him when I was in Cain Barber College in Chicago in 2004, and then he went on to start his own barber college, Chazap. Many of the other barbers that I attended Cain Barber College with always spoke very highly of Mr. D.

After my incident with the juvenile in Milwaukee, I came back home and did some refresher courses with Mr. D. at Chazap at the end of 2016. He understood the place that I was in emotionally and personally and became a confidant and mentor to me right away. He could empathize with me on so many levels. He was not only a teacher in the trade but a teacher in life - my *Obi-Wan Kenobi* in a sense.

When I was stressed, I was able to express myself to him and open up about the things that were bothering me. When I felt that I couldn't make it, he talked me *off the ledge* on more than one occasion. I could come to him whenever I needed some advice. He even helped me when I decided to pursue my civil suit against the Milwaukee School Board (which is still pending at the time of releasing this book). Or when other things in life didn't work out for me, he helped advise me through it. He was my Elisha Muhammed, and I was his Malcolm X, that's how close our bond was.

I'll never forget he was supposed to take me to my first Bonner Brothers Hair Show, but he got sick. Mr. D. wanted to expose me to more things in the barber world. He wanted me to experience life through a new lens and try to get away for the negativity that surrounded me because of my case. We had a ritual of going to our local Swamp-O-Rama (flea market) in a local Chicagoland suburb. We'd walk around and talk for hours, and then go out to eat afterward. He was a fun, lovable guy that I was forever grateful to have in my corner.

During the most critical moments of my life after the incident, he was there for me. I was completely devastated when he passed. Mr. D. had been a cancer survivor, but unfortunately, it ended up coming back. One of my last moments with Mr. D.

that I can remember is when he had me studying some Shakespeare literature as a way to enhance my acting. I don't know how much he knew about acting, but I felt like he was giving me a blessing to pursue it because he could see something in me.

This was an especially hard season for me because not only was I dealing with Mr. D. being ill, but a very close uncle to me was ill as well. They both died in the same year, and it really killed my spirits for a while. It was a sad day the day Mr. D. passed away. It was April 1, 2018, just so happened to be Easter and April Fool's Day. Mr. D's sister called us early Sunday morning to let us know that he had passed away. I remember that I was getting up to go to church, but after I heard the news, I was shocked. I couldn't move. I was hurt. For a while, I didn't want to accept that he was gone, but eventually, I had to move past it and keep moving because I know that he would have wanted me to. As much as he instilled in me, I know that he would have told me to keep my head lifted and carry out the purpose and mission that I was destined to complete.

On the day of Mr. D's visitation, I mustered up all the strength I could to go and see him, but I just couldn't bear seeing him in the casket. The pain was unbearable; especially after all that I'd been through in the last couple of years, losing my friend like that was heartbreaking. I remember after leaving the funeral home I went to the local bar and got really drunk, so drunk that the next day I had a really bad hangover. However, I knew I had to go and pay my last and final respect to my friend. I got to the funeral, and I can admit that I was a bit tipsy, but that was the only way I was going to make it through that service. I remember walking into this big beautiful church, and they had R. Kelly's *The World's Greatest* song playing in the service. Everyone had great words to say about Mr. D. I remember one man got up to talk about how Mr. D. was his superman, and he flew off the stage animated like to help us to really understand how much he felt like Mr. D. was his superman. I remember chuckling to myself about that.

Finally, it was my turn to get up to share words about my friend. I was a little nervous, and it definitely wasn't the easiest thing for me to do. I got up there on the stage and said, "How ya'll doing?" I went up there to tell my story about my friend, about

127

how much of a good person he was. Telling everyone of the beautiful spirit that he had and how much he'd been there for me. I thanked him over and over for his kindness toward me and how it was hard to let him go. It started to get real to me, and my emotions were starting to hit me. It was time for me to get off the stage because I didn't want to break down in tears in from of everyone. The ending tribute they played for Mr. D. was Mariah Carrey's song *Goodbye*. I walked up to that casket for the final goodbye and saluted Mr. D. We went to the burial, and I went home.

After Mr. D. passed away, I went into depression for a minute, and it was hard to come out of it for a while. I ended up going to the Bronner Brothers Hair Show in Atlanta, but it was very hard because that was supposed to be our trip. It was hard going to places that were specific to me and Mr. D. because it only brought back memories of him that I couldn't escape. I laugh because Mr. D. loved the waffle house. Mr. D. truly inspired me to be a better man in this world. I couldn't have faced the other half of my life these last couple of years without him. At the time of writing this book, it's been a year since his death, and I'm still representing Mr. D. He will forever live on in my heart.

I wrote this book because he always inspired me to tell my truth and live in my truth. I wouldn't be able to write this book had it not been for Mr. D. walking with me through recovery when I wanted to give up. I owe him so much more than just to live. I owe him by overcoming and being the best man I can be.

Peace

Made in the USA
Columbia, SC
09 March 2020